AKA "MY EMPIRE-ON-WHEELS PLANNER"

THE TRUCKING BIBLE CEO

WORKBOOK

STEPHANIE WILLIAMS, MBA

Entrepreneur | Strategic Business Consultant | Real Estate Investor and Mentor

BOOKED & BRANDED PUBLISHING

COPYRIGHT

Published by Booked and Branded Publishing
www.bookedandbrandedpublishing.com
ISBN: 978-1-969369-01-8

To inquire about licensing, speaking, or bulk orders, contact:

📩 hello@bookedandbrandedpublishing.com

TABLE OF CONTENTS

WELCOME **01**

How to Use This Planner

CHAPTER 1 **03**

Business Structure + Compliance Overview (continued)

CHAPTER 2 **05**

From Hustle to Legacy Reflection

CHAPTER 3 **07**

Freight Niches Brainstorm

TABLE OF CONTENTS

CHAPTER 4 09
Sales Scripts + Phone Pitch Notes

CHAPTER 5 11
Branding Your Business

CHAPTER 6 13
CEO Habits & Weekly Check-In

CHAPTER 7 15
Quote Wall + Power Prompts

FIND YOUR NEXT READ 17

TABLE OF CONTENTS

WORK WITH ME 19

FINAL NOTES 21

Let's turn your hustle into a legacy.

ABOUT THE AUTHOR 23

PRINTABLE TRACKER 24

WELCOME

How to Use This Planner

Welcome to your CEO Planning Workbook — your business brain in binder form. This isn't busywork — it's power strategy on paper.

Use this workbook to:

- Turn ideas into action plans
- Stay organized as you build your empire
- Keep your business vision front and center
- Document your growth like the boss you are

Recommended: Print it, keep it in a binder, or upload to a PDF-friendly app like GoodNotes.

CHAPTER 1

Business Structure + Compliance Overview (continued)

	YES	NO
EIN Registered		
Business Bank Account		
State Registration		
DOT Number Issued		
UCR Filed		
Insurance Active		

CHAPTER 2

From Hustle to Legacy Reflection

What's one "hustle" habit I'm ready to let go of?

What's one legacy-building habit I'm ready to adopt?

CHAPTER 3

Freight Niches Brainstorm

Top 3 freight niches I'm interested in:

1. ______________________________

2. ______________________________

3. ______________________________

What does success look like in this niche?

CHAPTER 4

Sales Scripts + Phone Pitch Notes

Sample Script:

"Hi, this is [Your Name] with [Your Company]. I'm calling to see if you have any loads available today for a [Truck Type] running [Route/Region]. We're reliable, fully compliant, and ready to roll."

Make it your own below:

CHAPTER 5

Branding Your Business

Brand Element	Your Notes
Company Name	
Logo Ideas	
Slogan / Tagline	
Brand Colors	
Social Handles	

What makes your company different?

CHAPTER 6

CEO Habits & Weekly Check-In

Habit	Rating (1–5)	Notes
Followed schedule		
Checked finances		
Communicated with team/drivers		
Took care of ME (self-care)		

CHAPTER 7

Quote Wall + Power Prompts

"You weren't born to blend in — you were born to build."

"My truck. My time. My terms."

"Generational wealth starts with uncomfortable decisions."

Your Affirmation of the Week:

Biggest win of the week:

FIND YOUR NEXT READ

Scan to explore more books like this one

WORK WITH ME

Want help building your business blueprint, launching your brand, or turning your knowledge into a bestselling book?

I specialize in strategy-backed ghostwriting and publishing for bold entrepreneurs who are ready to lead.

Website: www.bookedandbrandedpublishing.com

Email: hello@bookedandbrandedpublishing.com

Services:

- Ghostwriting
- Workbooks
- Publishing Support
- Business Strategy

FINAL NOTES

Let’s turn your hustle into a legacy.

Notes:

ABOUT THE AUTHOR

Stephanie Williams, MBA, is a Strategic Business Consultant, author, and powerhouse behind Booked and Branded Publishing. With over a decade of experience spanning corporate sales, real estate investment, and entrepreneurship, she brings unmatched clarity and confidence to every project.

Her expertise lies in transforming ideas into income — whether through premium ghostwriting, powerful branding, or step-by-step business building systems. Stephanie holds an MBA with a concentration in entrepreneurship from the Jack Welch Management Institute and has helped hundreds of professionals glow up their brands from the inside out.

Through her signature publishing and consulting firm, Stephanie empowers aspiring CEOs to turn their hustle into legacy — with strategy, speed, and style.

PRINTABLE TRACKER

Scan for printable tracker & digital copy

Made in the USA
Las Vegas, NV
03 November 2026

57420358R00019